Octopus Books

Portland & Denver

Published by Octopus Books
OctopusBooks.net

ISBN: 978-1-7334551-0-7

First Printing

HOW I BECAME A HUM
Eric Baus

CONTENTS

The Rain of the Ice

LOST MOAT

The injured octopus commandeered my limbs. It furrowed a crown of iron from its sponge dome but I felt no cruelty in the creature's cage. The wall of its body was more an annoyed wave. I was being guided, rained into a room where a tiny moon arose. I was being aired out, not raided. I touched the closest tentacle and felt a burned down candle. We were sharing an urn that was groomed for the cliffs. Moot and molting, we grabbed talons. We were born in a town around the block from our remains. We felt sad for our hands. We had loved our lost moat.

MUTE CASTING

The pupa's ghost escaped its octave. Begging to wander in a different cape, it walked until the distant, papery sound it was made from veered. It began to want a beast. It begat a llama. A shuddering strum. It became a walnut. It ate our rain.

STARVED SUN

The storming deer's pupils soaked themselves in milk. I watched its projected head. The amplified bulbs in the vatic branches arched until I saw nothing but the star.

DIAGRAMMED EAR

Whenever the diagrammed ear relents, forgetting its sound is the pupa's purpose. Bulbous, twinned in the grass, an O eggs itself, snowing.

ECHO SOLVENT

There is no wind, no blood, no sun. There is no sleep. Not water.
Not air. No capital, corpse, or crops. There are no wolves or waves.
No negative rain. Nor blue. Nor birds. No body.

THE SHORE GREW SAILS

The storm spored. The seeds split. The halves hatched. The snails unfurled. The shore poured over the waves. The cove reverted to grain.

WATER GRAZERS

I thought my silhouette had disappeared but the apparition emerged with ohms on its arms. It wrote a story with the remains of mayflies that redirected the river's pulse into the city's dirty body. We lived behind a dingy diorama. Underneath our tongue was the good ice. Inside of the snow was our head.

MICROPHONE MIND

The pupa collaged its rust. It sought a new hum. Renamed soot hid
in the drifts of its skin. It got microphone mind. It plumed.

AMBIENT CENTAUR

The agrarian century absorbed me into a horse. I was busy being a parable in a film about stormlessness. We watched the sun give birth to a lamp. We knelt to bury our glass in the sand.

ALPHA VAULT

The pupa condensed its peels with plumage. It unpacked an ambushed breath. It hid in the densest passage, wearing out the ether inside a downed cloud.

PAUSED DOPPEL

The day dried when my double's eyes opened. My other rewound his head. It is slowing inside my brother's rain. He said, "Test the mist. Say *Moon.* Wait. Say *Moon* with my spit." The wet remnants of his phonemes re-phased the scene. I did not die inside his delay. Our beeps released bees.

WORMS WERE STUCK TO HIS SÉANCE

The raw wings of a peregrine scared creases across his chest. Fox tracks fused his steps. Distant flares sparred in his eyes.

LACE SPECK

Being a size smaller than its call, the pupa balloons the surrounding cells. One mute note on a miniature string inflates the lace in a speck and its driftwood suit fills with silk.

THE RAIN OF THE ICE

The horse's pain never imagines a house beyond the storm. Its mirrored breath forms a force that dies without noise. The ice in a sickened room is not salt. Its perfume pours a rain that deletes the tacit skin.

Bad Shadow

The city convicted us of speaking through its horn. It said we reproduced a corrosive gloss. It scanned our accidents for invasive antlers. We undressed our shells in a sterile house. No one ever looked for us on 1515 Echo Lane.

The city wrote back to my brother. It said, "I would that the world began with a letter." "But what sort of world do I imply?" he asked, creating a system of dings in our diorama. His enjambed mouth reverberated in dirty space.

His voided voice unfolded. It unearthed a gauzy song. The verbs revealed themselves recursively through the moist, patient glass. We blurred our lenses. We implored our docents to implode but the constraints accrued. Hovering ministers distributed a coda.

My brother awoke from a bad shadow. He had stashed his hands in the snow. Aphids ate at his head. His ice forked to scatter its rain. The herd extracted static while wires grew through our grates. We watched the palms wave until our fingers froze.

Above all we were was a mirror. Much of our soil was gathered from conversation. Nothing is behind the screen. Our mouth was built entirely of redirected rivers. This caused a book of between, a house of plywood and polymers, a city we were never outside of.

The Datura Plains

WHAT OUR SKY IS LIKE

This was how we spoke to the distant flicker. Our silence hydrated a speaker. Its form came to us in pieces culled from the canopic night. We wore diagnostic dust in a book that believed only in ablutions. We dried slowly. Now what our sky is like is like a hospital for the sun.

THE SISTERS RODE ON

The sifters of the retracted path called out from several centuries away. They say they continued to disappear long after their blanked out footsteps first refused to register. The sisters rode on spindly deer, so light was the harvest and the whoosh of their habits.

LOOK AFTER OUR MIST

They thought their voices faintly until tiny droplets from the frozen canopy forged a worried skin. "Look after our mist," muttered the common cloud. Everyone inside them resounded the mesmerized room's movements. They heard themselves sway. Their refrain invaded a cicada din.

AN ANCESTRAL CUL-DE-SAC

The prior steeds were buried here a hundred cemeteries ago. The height of their extinguished crowns reached the knees of the clear-cut forest. They folded into a lone transitory foal for stalking sunning frogs. They preyed on teeth and burnt up beaks along an ancestral cul-de-sac.

THE GROUND ENGULFED US

We assembled our presence near the nervous stems. Our vows, movies. A shadow's babies. In this array, an injured shimmer rearranged. The gauze on the ground engulfed us. The most dismantled notes arose. I wanted to press record and sleep. I wanted to stay with my strangers.

Plan for a Lake on the Ceiling of a Cinema

SPEECH ORCHARD

We hid our hisses behind a bricked-over, whittled-out wind. It said our sounds only allowed us to begin: *itself, a sigh, a bee, the bees,* or *a slow retreat through snow.* The source reversed from wherever we had spoken into. It said, *say goodnight to the annexed voice,* and the pines burned our breath to survive.

OWLS IN THE WALLS

The city surrounded us for touching its hounds.

STROBE EGGS

My brother's lungs had synthesized a miniature sun. The swollen clouds collated. The blast's grammar washed through his flickering cells. He bore storming twins. They wore lead.

A BEAM IN THE ABYSS

Our interlaced heads collaborated on all stages of the reservoir's demise. We saw not what was sinking but what dissolved from being looked upon. The mannequin we proposed to evaporate our steps stopped short of its limbic training. It asked to be called A BEAM IN THE ABYSS. We simplified its spine. We cut into its centrifugal scarves. It cried.

SEAGULL MURMUR

Mice poured from an auxiliary skylight in the damaged heart of a guard dog. The sentry's brackets were bowing. Alloys from all nine injured frequencies contracted into a tungsten coat. A small tomato floated over its grave.

SUBMERGED PIANO PRESERVE

We compressed the resonance wounds inside an adult maple but the boom's drying thunder was buried under stones. Puréed hail bled from its tendrils. Swamp moss veiled the air.

FLOODED BULB

I felt a monsoon crown my brain when the circuits in the static sanctuary burst.

HOW WE DISGUISED CERTAIN OF OUR NOTES

We affixed our speakers to a dying sea. We purred out its pleas. We played THE MIRACLE OF THE WOLVES on an elephant's side. The tones propelled us through panicking krill.

THE FOREST FORMED GILLS

The ventriloquist's vines fled to an address on the floor of a cumulus pond. The forest formed gills. The tentacles muttered. *Eat a bee. Try to project the tiniest star deep beneath this fence.* The ravaged shadows repaired in the shade. The numb panorama rewound.

AUTONOMOUS INFIRMARY

The mirage minted its quills into a claw.

WRONG CLOAK

The calm squad blottered me and my brother's bulk into a gored together corpse. They lured an abscessed mop into whatever hurts form how we will be found. They sprayed WRONG CLOAK across the door to the datura plains and erased the space between clots. There I learned how lice can tame a mane. I learned that I was an intern pox for the crops to spurt loam from, but now I am training to be a glue ambassador for the corps. After another hour of helmeted breath, their clops returned to treeing peasants.

MYLAR COCOON

Huffing on a falcon while leaning in a lopsided tree, I fell into the ether-capped falls. I woke where all the swan eggs are copied from a single dead slug eye. The extinct oracle's seedlings reflected my tenor. Its tubers produced a bassoon.

WHEN HE WORE GNATS

I found him, in human sickness, marooned, a purse full of wasps,
the purest curse.

PLAN FOR A LAKE ON THE CEILING OF A CINEMA

The sudden ocean erased my feet. The coastline was curving away.
The raptors in the air formed a time-lapsed flash. The small moons
looped on mono. The surging birds coughed fur into my face while
our maps were put to sleep.

Wolfram Frock

But there we were, throbbing in an untraceable prism, thinking, *This is how milk wakes,* suspended above some adjunct hangman's jowls.

It was the era of the papier mâché robe, ancillary dusk, where a telegraph to the forest's front desk divides our Venn into two equidistant tufts.

My brother deployed a slight hatching sensation in our weather. The only way of knowing one of us had spoken was to watch the droplets gather on the glass.

We could read our respective doors: RAY ABATTOIR. MOON ROOM.

This is not speaking, he pled, in an effort to understand the vacuous process. There was something like feeling built into the blinds.

The condensation method tendered my head. It said, *You do not emit ownership. What I mean is, the rent in this room needs to be raised.*

We led our pawns through a series of furtive tracks. We tried to wear out the wolfram frock. We combined contaminants. It hurt.

People will say we colluded with a window. At some point, all the people will say, *So much for saliva. So much for elk.*

The Mesmerized Moth

I plagued myself in the moored room's waves. I forgot my flag.
I spooled. I wore a damaged mast. I swam the wall's face all day.

I swarmed a bolting watt. I horded its hairs. I watched the harm my claws compounded. I crowded beneath a harpsichord's lid.

I plucked the box's impacted strands. I mated scraps in a tiny stable. I pluralized its sod. I excerpted quakes. I ate a bite of paint.

I posed against the least wild light. I subtracted my effects. I rewired the flight of a flung piece of dust.

I, a sick leaf, awoke in scores. I plugged the grotto with séance paste. I dried calmly. I starred inside a new incense's whiff.

Autonomic Mica

BEGINNER'S ABYSS

Negative falcons plagued the flag. Each of their legs stored a small overturned tree. One ignited inside an expired cicada's cocoon. It dressed in its dimming twin's body until a skylight stashed below the forest floor smashed the crisis glass. Bouquets of aphids poured throughout the well-trained grave. What a choir of glue and borrowed glands. The scoured seed lured an abandoned antenna to sponge the steaming sea underground while the nascent beast coughed its brain into a commandeered cloud. No compass. No cove. No O.

REDACTED SECT

The school of the disassembling pulse. The school of the panicked tuft. The school of the soporific raft. The school of weightless darknesses. The school of almost nothing.

AUTOCHTHONIC WIRING

We weaved a vein of lava to put a pilot light beneath the defective plates, to sand down a redundant wave, to gauge the unseen sun's curse below our crops.

SUBLINGUAL CANDLE

The last star dissolved its heart into a simpler machine. Built from fox smoke and congealed cults, the glass eye let in a tiny lantern and all the snakes sparred with their shadows. It rose to revert to a letterless space, to hum beside the brook of sodden dressings, to wash beyond the storm-hatched lambs.

TAPE PRAYER

The confiscated hiss asked us to defect like we were only eyes paved into the lethal street or an emptying wreck revoking its shells but we were built of the polished shreds from a stretched out shroud. We had sworn to waft among dirges.

ANTIQUE MIASMA

The hour of buried lambs. The hour of revived lice. The hour of erased grass. The hour of the beginner's abyss.

AUTONOMIC MICA

Driftwood redistributed my brother's bones. An undetectable hymn disguised their sunken song until autonomic mica shadowed his brain. He awoke bolting between waves, disappeared but for the music combed into his clothes. My brother was a cup that doubled as a flood.

How I Became a Hum

MIRAGE REPAIR

The dead centaur's projected spleen secreted a dormant key. Its hide dredged an ingrown lion. The hours aged into a wave. The gallows weaved an illuminated egg.

TACIT FROG

The puma's pupils divided the horizon between a laminated cry and a starving creek. The void's traffic braided its spine into a corridor for radar. The delayed breath stretched a cough of milk through the tacit frog in a fish. The spores grew shale. The core camouflaged its frailty. The cloaked roar perfumed the eviscerated wind with a crystallized chorus of stares.

SEPIA STEAM

If the music in a film of ether flutters, this constitutes the sonic signature of the phantom power's flight. The result is a condensed dove.

THE ENTRANCED LEG

The sad boy buried a seed in his knee. The snail snored. The storm.
The shore. The storm. The shore. The mirror. The groan. The nerve
in the worm's core craned. *My shin wears a quail,* he cried.

EXALTED CLOTH

The pupa's lids wore blizzards until an errant rope panicked into hands. It wove archival quality ant salts but its sputtering organs soloed inanely. When the floor woke above its overdubbed bed the startled rubble administered stilts. It slid through its stitches. It spat a form of exalted cloth. Its itinerant skin dripped beginner's milk.

THE DEMILITARIZED MARIONETTE

The wooden arms unwound while the rabid trenches sweated. The ribboned fingers digested their threads. The doll distilled its bones beneath the hull of a bombed out mouse.

WOLF TONE

If the tongue's antonym remains occluded, a foot of debris gathers in its knot.

THE DECODED DRONE

The mirage's fugue bred orphan flames from film stills of the sun. The swarming shards mapped a redacted hand. The glued together tones grew scissors. The ghost of a blown up organ recorded its static in clotting fog.

GRID OASIS

The slug's pups strutted drunkenly between graves. The hoverers glazed on decaying glosses. They foraged among widows for a careless patch of grass.

PUPA DELUGE

Latent sleet in the cicada's soma rumbled. Combed into cramps, heaped beyond volume, the distorted quarters bubbled to uncoil.

THE BRAIN OF THE OX

The mirage's homonyms congested our antenna. Its ions addressed our grains. It said, *The history of a stem is another stem.* We reified our streams. We removed our atavistic lice with chips of flint. Isotopes exploded our scale.

REAPPEARER

The reverberation of a bursting whale departed the ocean's arcades. The novice corpse forged the outline of an eel from the vaporized worms in a bird. Its beakers grazed on satellite glass. Its gong germinated a squall.

COMPOUND MOUTH

The decoy voices amassed underground. *Our centuries share a phonetic bed*, scored the chorus.

HOW I BECAME A HUM

We mirrored the mirage's groans. We poured pollen into our microphones. We recorded our crops. We heard, *This is the city's apparatus minus the remains of a bell's hum.* We cracked the vatic eggs in our veins. We watched our eyes age. I split my thoughts. I was busy being a brook when a hidden atmosphere hatched. Then, the shore became my brains.

ACKNOWLEDGMENTS

Thanks to the editors of the following journals for publishing these poems: *Apartment, Connotation Press, Cloud Rodeo, Curious Specimen, Dreginald, Fence, Fruita Pulp, Handsome, Hobo, Inverted Syntax, Loose Change, Maggy, Map Points, Poets.org, Similar Peaks, Thermos, Wag's Revue.* The section "The Rain of the Ice" was published as a chapbook by above/ground press. Thanks to my friends, family, and teachers. Love to Andrea Rexilius, Marigold, and Virginia.

Cover image: Noah Saterstrom, *Levitation (2012)*
Cover image copyright © Noah Saterstrom
noahsaterstrom.com